THE LEFT-HANDED WOMAN

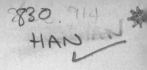

PETER HANDKE

Left-Handed Woman

Translated from the German by
RALPH MANHEIM

A Methuen Paperback

A Methuen Paperback

First published in Great Britain
by Eyre Methuen Ltd 1980
This edition published 1986
by Methuen London Ltd
11 New Fetter Lane, London EC4P 4EE
English translation copyright © 1977, 1978 by
Farrar, Straus and Giroux, Inc.
Originally published in German under the title
Die linkshändige Frau copyright © 1976 by
Suhrkamp Verlag, Frankfurt am Main
All rights reserved

Printed and bound in Great Britain
by Richard Clay (The Chaucer Press) Ltd,
Bungay, Suffolk

British Library Cataloguing in Publication Data

Handke, Peter
  The left-handed woman.
  I. Title II. Die linkshändige Frau.
  English
  833′.914[F] PT2668.A5

  ISBN 0-413-42390-5

This book is sold subject to the condition
that it shall not, by way of trade or otherwise,
be lent, resold, hired out or otherwise circulated
without the publisher's prior consent in any form
of binding or cover other than that in which
it is published and without a similar condition
including this condition being imposed
on the subsequent purchaser.

She was thirty and lived on an estate of bungalows laid out on the south slope of a low mountain range in western Germany, just above the fumes of a big city. She had brown hair and grey eyes, which sometimes lit up even when she wasn't looking at anyone, without her face changing in any other way. Late one winter afternoon she was sitting at an electric sewing machine, in the yellow light that shone into the large living room from outside. One entire side of the room consisted of a single pane of glass, looking out on the windowless wall of a neighbouring house and on a grass-overgrown terrace with a discarded Christmas tree in the middle of it. Beside the woman sat her eight-year-old son, bent over his exercise book, writing a school essay at a walnut table. His fountain pen scratched as he wrote, and his tongue protruded from between his lips. Now and then he stopped, looked out of the window, and went on writing more busily than ever. Or he would glance at his mother, who, though her face was averted, noticed his glance and returned it. The woman was married to the sales manager of the local branch of a porcelain manufacturer well known throughout Europe; a business trip had taken him to Scandinavia for several weeks, and he was expected back that evening. Though not rich, the family was comfortably well off, with no need to think of money. Their bungalow was rented, since the husband could be transferred at any moment.

The child had finished writing and read aloud: '"My idea of a better life. I would like the weather to be neither hot nor cold. There should always be a balmy breeze and once in a while a storm that makes people huddle on the ground. No more cars. All the houses should be red. The trees and bushes should be gold. I would know everything already, so I would not need to do lessons. Everybody would live on islands. The cars along the street would always be open, so I could get in if I happened to be tired. I would never be tired any more. They wouldn't belong to anyone. I would always stay up at night and fall asleep wherever I happened to be. It would never rain. I would always have four friends, and all the people I don't know would disappear. Everything I don't know would disappear." '

The woman stood up and looked out of the smaller side window. In the foreground a line of motionless pine trees. Below the trees several rows of individual garages, all as rectangular and flat-topped as the bungalows. The driveway leading to the garages had a pavement, and though it had been cleared of snow a child was pulling a sledge along it. Down in the lowland, far behind the trees, lay the outskirts of the city, and from somewhere in the hollow a plane was rising. The woman stood as if in a trance, but instead of going stiff she seemed to bend to her thoughts. The child came and asked her what she was looking at. She didn't hear him, she didn't so much as blink. The child shook her and cried, 'Wake up!' The woman came to, and put her hand on the child's shoulder. Then he, too, looked out and in turn lost himself, open-mouthed, in the view. After a while he shook himself and said, 'Now I've been woolgathering like you.' They both began to laugh and they couldn't stop; when their laughter died down, one started up again and the other joined in. In the end they hugged each other and laughed so hard they fell to the floor together.

The child asked if he could turn on the television. The woman answered, 'We're going to the airport now to meet Bruno.' But he was already turning on the set. The woman bent over him and said, 'Your father has been away for weeks. How can I tell him that ... ' The child heard nothing more. The woman made a megaphone with her hands and shouted as if she were calling him in the woods, but the child only

3

stared at the screen. She moved her hand back and forth in front of his eyes, but the child bent his head to one side and went on staring open-mouthed.

The woman stood in the space outside the garages in her open fur coat. Puddles of melted snow were freezing over. The pavement was strewn with the needles of discarded Christmas trees. While opening the garage door, she looked up at the estate and its tiers of box-shaped bungalows, some of which were already lighted. Behind the estate a mixed forest – mostly oaks, beeches, and pines – rose gently, unbroken by any village, or even a house, to the top of one of the mountains. The child appeared at the window of their 'housing unit', as her husband called the bungalow, and raised his arm.

At the airport it wasn't quite dark yet; before going into the terminal, the woman saw bright spots in the sky over the flagpoles with their shimmering flags. She stood with the others and waited, her face expectant and relaxed, open and self-possessed. Word came over the loudspeaker that the plane from Helsinki had landed, and soon the passengers emerged from behind the customs barrier, among them Bruno, carrrying a suitcase and a plastic bag marked 'Duty-Free Shop'. He was just a little older than she, and his face was drawn with fatigue. He wore, as always, a double-breasted grey pin-striped suit and an open shirt. His eyes were so brown that it

4

was hard to see his pupils; he could watch people for a long time without their feeling looked at. He had walked in his sleep as a child, and even now he often talked in his dreams.

In front of all the people, he rested his head on the shoulder of his wife's fur coat, as if he had to take a nap that minute. She took his suitcase and plastic bag, and then he was able to throw his arms around her. For a long time they stood embracing; Bruno smelled slightly of drink.

In the lift that took them to the underground garage, where she had parked, he looked at her and she observed him. She got into the car first and opened the door from inside. Instead of getting in, he stood looking straight ahead. He beat his forehead with his fist; then he held his nose and tried to blow air out of his ears, as though they were still blocked after the long flight.

On the road to the small town on the mountain slope where the bungalows were, the woman put her hand on the radio knob and asked, 'Would you like some music?' He shook his head. By then it was dark; nearly all the lights were out in the high-rise office buildings along the road, but the housing estates on the hills were bright.

After a while Bruno said, 'It was always so dark in Finland – day and night. And I couldn't understand a single word of the language! In every other country

5

a few of the words are similar – but there's nothing international about that language. The one thing I've remembered is the word for beer – *"olut"*. I got drunk fairly often. Early one afternoon, when just a little light had come into the sky, I was sitting in a self-service café. All at once I began to scratch the table in a frenzy. The darkness, the cold in my nostrils, and not being able to speak to anyone. It was almost comforting to hear the wolves howl one night. Or to pee into a lavatory with our company's initials on it. There's something I've been wanting to tell you, Marianne. I thought of you often up there, of you and Stefan. For the first time in all the years since we've been together, I had the feeling that we belonged to each other. Suddenly I was afraid of going mad with loneliness, mad in a cruelly painful way that no one had ever experienced before. I've often told you I loved you, but now for the first time I feel that we're bound to each other. Till death do us part. And the strange part of it is that I now feel I could exist without you.'

The woman rested her hand on Bruno's knee and asked, 'And how did the business go?'

Bruno laughed. 'Orders are picking up again,' he said. 'Those northerners may not eat very well, but at least they eat off our china. The next time, our Finnish customers will have to come down here and see us. The prices have stopped falling: we don't have

to give such big discounts as we did during the crisis.'
He laughed again. 'They don't even speak English.
We had to talk through an interpreter, a woman with
a child and no husband, who studied in Germany – in
the south, I think.'

The woman: 'You think?'

Bruno: 'No, of course not. I know. She told me.'

After putting the car away they walked past a
lighted telephone box with a shadowy form moving
about inside, and turned into one of the narrow,
deliberately crooked lanes that cut across the estate.
He put his arm over her shoulders. While opening the
door of their house, the woman looked back at the
half-dark lane and the tiers of bungalows, all with
their curtains drawn.

Bruno asked, 'Do you still like it here?'

The woman: 'Sometimes I wish we had a smelly
pizza place outside the door, or a news-stand.'

Bruno: 'I know I'm always relieved to get back.'

The woman smiled to herself.

In the living room the child was sitting in a big,
broad armchair, reading by the light of a standing
lamp. He looked up for a moment when his parents
came in. Bruno stepped close to him, but he didn't
stop reading. Finally he smiled almost imperceptibly,
stood up, and searched Bruno's pockets for presents.

The woman came from the kitchen, carrying a
silver tray with a glass of vodka on it, but by then

there was no one in the living room. She went down the hall and looked into the rooms that branched off it like cells. When she opened the bathroom door, Bruno was sitting motionless on the rim of the tub, watching the child, who was already in his pyjamas, brush his teeth. The child had rolled up his sleeves to keep the water from running into them. He carefully licked the toothpaste from the open tube and then, standing on tiptoe, put the tube back on the shelf. Bruno took the glass of vodka from the tray and asked, 'Aren't you drinking anything? Have you made any plans for the evening?'

The woman: 'Why? Am I different from usual?'

Bruno: 'You're always different.'

The woman: 'What do you mean by that?'

Bruno: 'You're one of the few people I don't have to be afraid of. What's more, you don't make me want to play-act.' He sent the child away with an affectionate pat.

In the living room, as they were picking up the toys the child had been playing with that day, Bruno stood up and said, 'My ears are still buzzing from the plane. Let's go to the hotel for a celebration dinner. It's too private here for me just now. Too – haunted. I would like you to wear your low-cut dress.'

The woman was still squatting on the floor, picking up toys. 'What will you wear?' she asked.

Bruno: 'I'll go just as I am. I always do. I'll borrow

a tie at the reception desk. I feel like walking. All right?'

The hotel restaurant, whose lofty ceiling gave it a palatial look, was half empty. Bruno was still adjusting his tie as they walked into the dining room, guided by a bow-legged waiter. The headwaiter pulled out chairs for them, and they had only to let themselves sink down. They unfolded their white napkins in unison and laughed.

Bruno not only ate everything on his plate but wiped the plate clean with a piece of bread. Afterwards, holding up and gazing into a glass of Calvados, which took on a reddish glow in the light of the chandeliers, he said, 'Tonight I felt the need of being served like this! How sheltered one feels! A taste of eternity!' The headwaiter stood in the background as Bruno continued. 'I read an English novel on the plane. There's a passage about a butler who combines dignity with eagerness to serve. The hero watches him and meditates on the mature beauty of the feudal master-servant relationship. To be waited on in this proud, respectful way, if only for a brief moment at tea, reconciles him not only with himself but also, in some strange way, with the whole human race.' The woman turned away; Bruno spoke to her, and she turned back but did not look at him.

Bruno said, 'We'll spend the night here. Stefan

knows where we are. I left the telephone number on his bedside table.' The woman lowered her eyes and Bruno motioned to the waiter, who bent over him. 'I need a room for the night,' he said. 'You see, my wife and I want to sleep together right away.'

The waiter smiled. There was nothing conspiratorial, only sympathy in the way he looked at them. 'There's a trade fair on at the moment, but I'll inquire,' he said. At the door he turned around and added, 'I'll be back in a moment.'

The two were alone in the dining room. Candles were still burning on all the tables, and around them needles were falling almost soundlessly from sprays of evergreen. Shadows moved over the tapestries of hunting scenes on the walls. The woman gave Bruno a long look. Though she was very grave, her face lit up almost imperceptibly.

The waiter came back and said in a voice that sounded as if he had been hurrying, 'Here is the key to the tower room. Statesmen have slept there, but I'm sure you see no harm in that.' Bruno dismissed the waiter's remark with a wave of the hand, and without seeming offensive the waiter added, 'I wish you a very good night. I hope the tower clock doesn't disturb you; you see, the big hand purrs every minute.'

As Bruno opened the door to the room, he said very calmly, 'Tonight I feel as if everything I'd ever wished for had come true. As though I could move by magic from one place of happiness to another, without transition. I feel a magic power, Marianne. And I need you. And I'm happy. Everything inside me is buzzing with happiness.' He smiled at her, and there was surprise in his smile. They went in and switched on all the lights – in the vestibule and bathroom as well as the bedroom.

In the first grey of dawn the woman was awake. She looked towards the window, which was partly open; the curtains were parted, and the winter fog was blowing in. The minute hand purred softly. She said to Bruno, who was sleeping beside her, 'I want to go home.'

He understood her instantly, in his sleep.

They walked slowly down the path leading out of the park. Bruno had his arm around her. After a while he ran ahead and turned a somersault on the hard-frozen turf.

The woman stopped walking and shook her head. Bruno, who had gone on a little way, looked back questioningly. She said, 'Nothing, nothing at all,' and again shook her head. She stood looking at Bruno, as though looking at him helped her to think. Then he came back to her. Turning away from him, she looked at the frost-covered trees and bushes,

11

which were briefly shaken by the morning breeze.

The woman said, 'I've had a strange idea. Well, not really an idea, more like an - illumination. But I don't want to talk about it. Let's go home now, Bruno. Quickly. I have to drive Stefan to school.'

Bruno stopped her. 'Woe if you don't tell me.'

The woman: 'Woe to you if I do tell you.'

Even as she spoke, she couldn't help laughing at the strange word they had used. The long look they exchanged was mocking at first, then nervous and frightened, and finally resigned.

Bruno: 'All right. Out with it.'

The woman: 'I suddenly had an illumination' - another word she had to laugh at - 'that you were going away, that you were leaving me. Yes, that's it. Go away, Bruno. Leave me.'

After a while Bruno nodded slowly, raised his arms in a gesture of helplessness, and asked, 'For good?'

The woman: 'I don't know. All I know is that you'll go away and leave me.' They stood silent.

Bruno smiled and said, 'Well, first I'll just go back to the hotel and get myself a cup of hot coffee. And this afternoon I'll come and take my things.'

There was no malice in the woman's answer - only thoughtful concern. 'I'm sure you can move in with Franziska for the first few days. Her teacher friend has gone away.'

Bruno: 'I'll think about it over my coffee.' He went back to the hotel.

In the long avenue leading out to the estate she took a hop step and suddenly started to run. At home she opened the curtains, switched on the record player, and started making dance movements even before the music began. The child appeared in his pyjamas and asked, 'What are you doing?'

The woman: 'I think I'm depressed.' And then, 'Dress yourself, Stefan. It's time for school. I'll be making your toast in the meantime.' She went to the hall mirror and said, 'Christ ... Christ ... Christ.'

It was a bright winter morning; the mist, which was breaking up, shed an occasional snowflake. Outside the school the woman met her friend Franziska, who was also Stefan's teacher, a solidly built woman with short blonde hair and a voice that made itself heard in the midst of any gathering, even when she wasn't raising it. She was always expressing opinions, less from conviction than for fear that her conversation might otherwise be thought trivial.

The school bell had just begun to ring. Franziska greeted the child with a slap on the back and said to the woman as he vanished in the doorway, 'I know all about it. Bruno phoned me right away. Do you know what I said to him? "At last your Marianne has woken up." Is that how you feel? Are you really serious?'

The woman: 'I can't talk now, Franziska.'

13

The teacher started into the building and called back, 'Meet me at the café after school. I'm so excited.'

The woman emerged from the dry cleaner's carrying bundles; queued at the butcher's; in the car park of the town supermarket stowed heavy plastic shopping bags in the back seat of her Volkswagen. Then, with still a bit of time to kill, she walked around the big, hilly park, past frozen ponds with a few ducks sliding about on them. She wanted to sit down somewhere, but the seats of all the benches had been removed for the winter. And so she stood looking at the cloudy sky. Some elderly people stopped near her, and they, too, looked at the sky.

She met Franziska at the café; the child sat beside her reading a comic book. Franziska pointed at the book and said, 'That duck is the only comic-book character I tolerate in my class. I even encourage my pupils to read his sad adventures. They learn more about real life from this eternal victim than they could from anyone else in this home-owner's paradise, where all existence boils down to imitating TV.' The woman and the child behind the comic book exchanged glances.

Franziska: 'And what will you do now that you're on your own?'

The woman: 'Sit at home biting my nails.'

Franziska: 'No, seriously. Is there someone else?'

14

The woman only shook her head.

Franziska: 'What will the two of you live on? Have you thought of that?'

The woman: 'No. But I'd like to start translating again. At the publishing house where I used to work, I only had foreign rights contracts to deal with. But when I left, the boss said I could do proper books. He's been making me offers ever since.'

Franziska: 'Novels. Poems! Good God! I bet they'll pay you twenty marks a page. Maybe three marks an hour.'

The woman: 'I believe it's fifteen marks a page.'

Franziska gazed at her. 'I do wish you'd come to our group soon. You'll see. When we get together, every single one of us comes to life. And we don't exchange recipes! You have no idea how blissful women can be together.'

The woman: 'I'll be glad to come sometime.'

Franziska: 'Have you ever lived alone?'

When the woman shook her head again, Franziska said, 'I have. And I despise it. I despise myself when I'm alone. Oh, by the way, Bruno will stay at my place for the present – unless you take him back this afternoon, which wouldn't surprise me. I still can't believe it all. But I'm delighted all the same, Marianne, and in some strange way I'm proud of you.'

She drew the woman to her and embraced her.

Then she gave the child, behind the comic book, a tap on the knee and asked, 'How does moneybags fleece his poor relation this time?' Immersed in his reading, the child didn't react, and for a long time no one spoke. Then the woman said, 'Stefan always wants to be the rich one – he says he's the better man.'

Franziska raised her empty glass to her lips and went through the motions of drinking. She put the glass down and looked back and forth between woman and child. Little by little, her features softened. (That was Franziska's way. Sometimes, for no particular reason, she would suddenly melt into speechless tenderness and her face, relaxing, would take on a likeness to the faces of many other, very different women – as though in this undirected tenderness she discovered herself.)

At home, in the hallway of the bungalow, the wall cupboards were open, and the woman was getting ready to pack Bruno's bags. The suitcases were on the floor in front of her, and when she opened one of them she found the child curled up inside; he jumped up and ran away. From a second suitcase popped one of Stefan's friends, a rather fat little boy named Jürgen, who followed him out onto the terrace. There they pressed their faces against the window and stuck out their tongues, which instantly felt the sting of the ice-cold glass. On her knees in the hallway, the woman carefully folded Bruno's shirts. Then she dragged the suitcases into the living room, and left them there, all ready to be called for. When the bell rang, she hurried into the kitchen. Bruno walked in, and looked around like an intruder. He saw the suitcases, called his wife, and, pointing at them, said with a grin, 'Have you taken my picture off the bedside table?'

They took each other's hands.

He asked what Stefan was doing, and she motioned towards the big window, behind which the two children were silently making faces.

After a while Bruno said, 'Isn't it strange what happened to us this morning? And neither of us was drunk. Now I feel rather silly. Don't you?'

The woman: 'Yes, I suppose so. Well, no, not really.'

Bruno took the suitcases. 'It's a good thing the office opens up again tomorrow ... You've never lived alone.'

The woman: 'So you've come from Franziska?' And then she said, 'Don't you want to sit down?'

On his way out Bruno shook his head and said, 'You take it so lightly ... Do you remember that there was once a closeness between us that may have been based on the fact of our being man and wife but went far beyond it?'

The woman shut the door behind him and stood

there. She heard the car driving off; she went to the coat-rack beside the door and thrust her head among the coats.

As the dusk deepened, the woman did not turn on the light but sat looking at the television screen. Their set had a special channel for watching the estate's playground. The silent black-and-white image revealed her son balancing himself on a tree trunk, while his fat friend kept falling off; except for the two of them, the playground was foresaken. The woman's eyes glistened with tears.

The woman and the child took their supper alone in the living room. She had already finished and was watching the child, who guzzled and smacked his lips. Otherwise, it was very still, except now and then for the buzzing of the refrigerator in the kitchen, which was connected with the living room by a service hatch. There was a telephone at the woman's feet.

She asked Stefan if she should put him to bed. He answered, 'I always put myself to bed.'

The woman: 'Let me come with you at least.'

To the child's surprise she helped him into his pyjamas. Then she tried to pick him up and put him into bed. He resisted and climbed in by himself, whereupon she pulled up the blankets and tucked

18

him in. He was holding a book, and pointed out a picture in it, showing high mountains in a bright light; jackdaws were flying about in the foreground. He read the legend under the picture aloud: '"Mountain scene in late autumn: Even at this time of year the summits beckon if the weather cooperates."' He asked her what it meant and she translated; it meant you could still go mountain-climbing in late autumn if the weather was good. She bent over him and he said, 'You smell of onions.'

Alone in the kitchen, the woman crouched over the rubbish bin. She was holding the child's plate, which still had some food on it, and she had her foot on the pedal of the bin, so that the lid was already raised. Still bent over, she forked a few morsels into her mouth, chewed them, and tossed what was left into the bin. Then for a time she remained motionless in the same posture.

That night, lying on her back in bed, she opened her eyes wide. There was no sound to be heard but her breath against the bedclothes and a suspicion of her pounding heart. She went to the window and opened it, but the silence only gave way to a soft murmur. She carried her blanket into the child's room and lay down on the floor beside his bed.

One morning some days later the woman sat typing

in the living room. In an undertone she read what she had written: '"I am finally in a position to consider your repeated offers of translation from the French. Please let me know of your conditions. At the moment I should prefer non-fiction. I have a pleasant memory of my days in your office"' - to herself, she added 'in spite of the sprained wrists I was always getting from typing all day' - '"and look forward to hearing from you."'

She threw the letter into the post-box beside the telephone box on the edge of the estate. When she turned away, Bruno was coming towards her. He seized her roughly by the arm, then looked around to see if anyone was watching. Up the road an elderly couple equipped for hiking - knickerbockers, knapsacks, and walking sticks - had turned round. Bruno pushed the woman into the phone box. Then suddenly he apologised.

He gave her a long look. 'Do we have to go on with this game, Marianne? I, for one, am sick of it.'

The woman replied, 'Now, don't start talking about the child.'

He struck out, but the phone box was too cramped, and he didn't really hit her. He raised his hands as though to bury his face in them, but let them drop. He said, 'Franziska thinks you don't know what you're doing. She says you have no inkling of the historical conditions that determine your conduct.' He laughed. 'Do you know what she says you are? A private mystic. She's right. You *are* a mystic. Damn it, you're not well. I told Franziska a bit of electro-shock would straighten you out.'

After a long silence the woman said, 'Of course you can come and see us whenever you like – on weekends, for instance – and take Stefan to the zoo. Or the Historical Museum.'

Another silence. Suddenly Bruno produced a photograph of her, held it up, and then set fire to it with his lighter. She tried not to smile and looked at something else; then she smiled after all.

Bruno left the phone box and threw the burning photograph away; she followed him. He looked around and said calmly, 'What about me? Do you think I don't exist? Do you suppose there's no one else in the world but you? I exist, too, Marianne. I exist!'

At this moment the woman pulled Bruno, who had started to wander off into the roadway, out of the path of a car.

Bruno asked, 'Do you need money?' and took out some banknotes.

The woman: 'We have a joint account, you know. Or have you closed it?'

'Of course not. But take this anyway, even if you don't need it. Please.' He held out the money, and in the end she took it, after which they both seemed relieved. In leaving, he sent Stefan his love. She nodded and said she would visit him soon in his office.

When he had walked quite a way, Bruno called back over his shoulder. 'Don't be alone too much. It could be the death of you.'

At home the woman stood at the hall mirror and looked into her eyes – not to see anything special but as a way of thinking about herself calmly.

She spoke out loud. 'I don't care what you people think. The more you have to say about me, the freer I will be of you. Sometimes I have the impression that the moment we discover something new about a person it stops being true. From now on, if anyone tells me what I'm like, even if it's to flatter or encourage me, I'll take it as an insult and refuse to listen.' She stretched out her arms. There was a hole in her sweater, under one armpit; she stuck her finger into it.

All of a sudden she started moving the furniture. The child helped her. When they had finished, they stood in different corners of the living room, surveying the new arrangement. Outside, it was raining – a furious winter rain that bounced off the hard ground like hail. The child pushed the carpet sweeper in all directions; bareheaded on the terrace, the woman cleaned the big window with old newspapers. She squirted spot-remover foam on the carpet. She threw bags and books into a plastic refuse bag standing beside other bags that had already been tied up. She took a rag and polished the letter-box outside the door; she placed a ladder under the living-room light, climbed up, unscrewed a bulb, and put in a much stronger one.

That evening the room was resplendent. The walnut table, now covered with a white tablecloth, was set for two; in the centre a thick yellow beeswax candle was burning, and the wax sizzling audibly. The child folded the napkins and placed them on the plates. To the sound of soft dinner music ('dinner music in the housing unit', as Bruno had put it), they sat down facing each other. As they unfolded their napkins in unison, the woman gasped, and the child asked if she was depressed again. She shook her head for a long time, in negation but also in surprise; then she took the lid off the serving dish.

During the meal the child told her the latest news: 'Listen to what happened at school. Our class took off their coats and boots and put on their slippers and school overalls in four minutes flat. The principal times us with a real stopwatch. It took us ten minutes at the beginning of the term. The principal said we could easy get it down to three minutes by the end of the year. We'd have done it today if that fat Jürgen hadn't got all tangled up in his coat buttons. And then he cried all morning. At playtime he went and hid in the cloakroom and peed in his pants. You know how we'll make it in three minutes? We'll start running at the top of the stairs and take everything off before we get there.'

The woman said, 'So that's why you always want to wear your light coat in spite of the cold – because it's easier to unbutton!' She laughed.

The child: 'Don't laugh like that. You laugh like fat Jürgen. He always knocks himself out trying to laugh. You're never really pleased. You were only pleased with me once – that time when we were bathing and all of a sudden I came swimming up to you without my ring around me. You picked me up and you were so happy you were screaming.'

The woman: 'I don't remember.'

The child: 'But I remember.' And he shouted malignantly, 'I remember! I remember!'

That night the woman sat by the window with the curtains drawn, reading; a thick dictionary lay beside her. She put her book aside and opened the curtains. A car was just turning into one of the garages, and on the pavement an elderly lady was walking her dog. As though nothing escaped her, she looked up at the window and waved.

*

The woman pushed her trolley down one of the narrow aisles of the supermarket; if someone came along in the opposite direction, she had to turn into a side passage. Empty trolleys jangled as a shop assistant collected them; a handbell was rung at the bottle-return window; the muzak was interrupted again and again by announcements of the bargains of the day, week, and month. For a time the woman stood motionless, looking around her more and more calmly; her eyes began to shine.

In a quieter aisle she ran into Franziska, who was pulling her trolley behind her.

Franziska: 'At the bread counter just now I saw them wrapping a loaf for a local woman; a Yugoslav came next and they just handed his to him unwrapped ... I usually go to the grocer on corner, even if his salad is half withered or fr But I can't afford such philanthropy every d

Both were jostled, and the woman sai times I feel good in this place.'

Franziska pointed to a peephole in partition, behind which a man in a watching the customers. She had herself heard above the noise. 'I corpse gives you a sense of se

The woman: 'He's right fo the supermarket is right f

As they queued at the

the woman's elbow and said with an air of embarrassment, 'I bet we've picked the wrong queue. We'll still be waiting when all those people on the right and left are on their way home. It happens to me every time.'

Outside the supermarket a number of dogs were tied up and shivering with cold. Franziska took the woman's arm. 'Please come to our group meeting tomorrow night. They'll all be so glad to have you. Just at the moment they have a feeling that human thought is in pretty good shape but that life is ~~here. We need someone who's making a bit of a ~~ normal way of life – in other words, ~~You know what I mean.'

~~like to be alone in the

~~the
~~zen.
~~ay.', 'Some-
~~a polystyrene
~~hite smock sat'
~~o shout to make
~~suppose that living
~~urity?'
~~r the supermarket. And
~~or me. Today, at least.'
~~heckout, Franziska stroked

25

in
g

he
e a
dn't

e, try
men at

As the woman set off for the car park, Franziska called after her, 'Don't take to solitary drinking, Marianne.'

The woman moved on with her plastic shopping bags. One of the handles tore, and she had to hold her hand underneath the bottom.

In the evening the woman and the child sat watching television. The child finally jumped up and switched off the set. Confused and surprised, the woman said, 'Oh, thank you,' and rubbed her eyes.

The doorbell rang; the child ran and answered it. Feeling a little dizzy, the woman stood up. Through the open door bustled the publisher she had worked for, a heavyset but rather fidgety man of fifty, who when talking to someone had a way of coming closer and closer and assuming a slight foreign accent. (He always seemed concerned about something, and unbent only when made to feel that he didn't have to prove himself. A meeting with even his closest friends made him jumpy, as if he had just been awakened out of a deep sleep and wouldn't be himself until fully awake. Wherever he happened to be, he behaved as if he were the host, and only if his interlocutor failed to react did his sociability, made truly disconcerting by his visible efforts to keep it going, give way to a relaxed composure in which he seemed to be resting from his constant need to communicate.)

He had flowers in one hand and a bottle of champagne in the other.

He said, 'I knew you were alone, Marianne. When a publisher gets a letter, he has to know how to read between the lines.' He handed her his offerings. 'Ten years! Do you still recognise me? I, at least, remember every detail of the farewell party we gave you at the office, Marianne. I especially remember a certain smell of lilies of the valley behind a certain ear.'

The child stood listening. The woman asked, 'And what do you smell today?' The publisher sniffed the air.

The woman: 'It's Brussels sprouts. The smell lingers in the cupboards for days. But it's one vegetable that children like. I'll get two glasses for the bubbly.'

The publisher cried out, 'Don't say "bubbly." Say "champagne"!' And quickly, in a different tone, 'How do you say "Brussels sprouts" in French?'

The woman said, *'Choux de Bruxelles.'*

The publisher clapped his hands. 'You pass. You see, I've brought you the autobiography of a young Frenchwoman. Naturally it's full of such words. You can start translating tomorrow.'

The woman: 'Why not tonight?'

The publisher: 'The lilies of the field didn't work at night.'

The woman: 'Why bring them in?'

'I suppose I was thinking of those lilies of the valley.'

The woman only smiled. 'Will you open the bottle?' She went to the kitchen with the flowers. The publisher tugged at the champagne cork. The child watched.

They sat in the living room drinking. The child had a few sips too. After a festive clinking of glasses, the woman caressed the child and the publisher said, 'I had to come out here anyway. One of my authors lives in the neighbourhood. I'm worried about him. A difficult case. He's stopped writing. For good, I'm afraid. The publishing house is helping him out, of course. We've been irresponsibly generous. This evening I was urging him to write his autobiography at least – autobiographies are in great demand. But he only shook his head. He won't talk to anyone any more; he only makes noises. He has a ghastly old age ahead of him, Marianne. No work, no friends.'

The woman replied with a strange violence, 'You don't know anything about him. Maybe he's happy some of the time.'

The publisher turned to the child. 'Now you're going to see some magic. I'm going to make that cork disappear from the table.' The child looked at the table. The publisher pointed one hand up in the air and said, 'There it goes.' But the child kept his eyes glued to the cork, and the publisher dropped his arm. He said quickly to the woman, 'Why do you defend the man?'

As though in answer, the woman tickled the child, kissed him on the head, picked him up, put him on her lap, hugged him.

The publisher: 'Don't you like my company? I have the impression that you keep so busy with the child only so you won't have to pay any attention to me. What's the sense of this mother-and-child game? What have you to fear from me?'

The woman pushed the child away and said, 'Maybe you're right,' and to the child, 'Go to bed.'

The child didn't move, so she picked him up and carried him off.

She came back alone and said, 'Stefan doesn't want to sleep. The champagne makes him think of New Year's Eve, when he can always stay up until past midnight.' The publisher drew the woman down beside him on the broad armchair; with an air of forbearance she let him.

The publisher said slowly, 'Which is your glass?'

She showed him and he picked it up. 'I want to drink out of your glass, Marianne.'

Then he smelled her hair. 'I like your hair because it only smells of hair. It's more a feeling than a smell. And another thing I like is the way you walk. It's not a special kind of walk, as with most women.

You just walk, and that's lovely.'

The woman smiled to herself. Then she turned to him as though a sudden desire to talk had come over her. 'One day a lady was here. She played with Stefan. All of a sudden he sniffed at her hair and said, "You smell." The woman was horrified. "Of cooking?" she cried. "No, of perfume," he said, and that relieved her completely.'

After a while the publisher looked at her as if he didn't know what to do next. The child called her, but she did not respond. She looked back towards his room as though curious. The publisher kept his eyes on her but lowered his head. 'You've got a ladder.' She waved her hand, meaning she didn't care, and when the child called her again she stood up but didn't leave the room.

She sat down in her old place, across from the publisher, and said, 'What I can't bear in this house is the way I have to turn corners to go from one room to another: always at right angles and always to the left. I don't know why it puts me in such a bad mood. It really torments me.'

The publisher said, 'Write about it, Marianne. One of these days you won't be with us any more if you don't.'

The child called a third time and she went to him instantly.

Left alone, the publisher looked tired. His head

sagged slightly to one side. He straightened up; then he smiled, apparently at himself, and let his body go limp again.

The woman came back and stood in front of him. He looked up at her. She laid her hand on his forehead. Then she sat down across from him again. He took her hand, which was resting on the table, and kissed it. For a long time they said nothing.

She said, 'Should I play some music for you?' He shook his head without a moment's reflection, as though he had expected the question. They were silent.

The publisher: 'Doesn't your telephone ever ring?'

The woman: 'Very seldom in the last few days. Not much in the winter, anyway. Maybe in the spring?' After a long silence she said, 'I think Stefan is asleep now.' And then, 'If you weren't my boss now, in a manner of speaking, I might let you see how tired I am.'

The publisher: 'And besides, the bottle is empty.'

He got up and she saw him to the door. He took his coat, stood with bowed head, then straightened up. Brusquely she took his coat out of his hands and said, 'Let's have another glass. I've just had a feeling that every minute I spend alone I lose something that can never be retrieved. Like death. Forgive the word. It was a painful feeling. Please don't misunderstand me. There's still a bottle of red Burgundy in the kitchen. It's a heavy wine, it puts you to sleep.'

They stood by the living-room window, drinking the red wine. The curtains were open, and they looked out into the garden; snow was falling.

The publisher said, 'Not long ago I broke with a girl I loved. The way it happened was so strange that I'd like to tell you about it. We were riding in a taxi at night. I had my arm around her, and we were both looking out the same side. Everything was fine. Oh yes, you have to know that she was very young – no more than twenty – and I was very fond of her. For the barest moment, just in passing, I saw a man on the pavement. I couldn't make out his features, the street was too dark. I only saw that he was rather young. And suddenly it flashed through my mind that the sight of that man outside would force the girl beside me to realise what an old wreck was holding her close, and that she must be filled with revulsion. The thought came as such a shock that I took my arm away. I saw her home, but at the door of her house I told her I never wanted to see her again. I bellowed at her. I said I was sick of her, it was all over between us, she should get out of my sight. And I walked off. I'm certain she still doesn't know why I left her. That young man on the pavement probably didn't mean a thing to her. I doubt if she even noticed him ...'

He drained his glass. They stood silently, looking out of the window. The woman with the dog

33

appeared, looked up, and waved; she was carrying an open umbrella.

The publisher said, 'It's been a beautiful evening, Marianne. No, not beautiful – different.'

They went to the door.

The publisher: 'I shall take the liberty of making your phone ring now and then, even in the dead of winter.'

He put on his coat. In the doorway she asked him if he had come in his car; the snow was swirling into the house.

The publisher: 'Yes. With a chauffeur. He's waiting in the car.'

The woman: 'You let him wait all this time?'

The publisher: 'He's used to it.'

The car was outside the door, the chauffeur sitting in the half-darkness.

The woman: 'You've forgotten to give me the book I'm to translate.'

The publisher: 'I left it in the car.'

He motioned to the chauffeur, who brought in the book.

The publisher handed it to the woman, who asked, 'Were you putting me to the test?'

The publisher, after a pause: 'You're entering on a period of long loneliness, Marianne.'

The woman: 'Everybody has been threatening me lately.' And to the chauffeur, who was standing beside them, 'What about you? Are you threatening me, too?' The chauffeur smiled uncomfortably.

That night she stood alone in the hall with the book. The snow crackled on the skylights in the flat roof overhead. She began to read: *'Au pays de l'idéal: J'attends d'un homme qu'il m'aime pour ce que je suis et pour ce que je deviendrai.'* She attempted a translation: 'In the land of the ideal: I expect a man to love me for what I am and for what I shall become.' She shrugged.

In broad daylight she sat at the table with her typewriter in front of her, and put on her glasses. She divided the book she was to translate into daily quotas of pages, and after each quota she wrote the corresponding date in pencil; by the end of the book she had arrived at a date in mid-spring. Haltingly, stopping to leaf through the dictionary, to clean a letter on the typewriter with a needle, to wipe the keys with a cloth, she wrote the following passage: 'Up until now all men have weakened me. My husband says: "Michèle is strong." The truth is that he wants me to be strong in connection with things that don't interest him: the children, the household, taxes. But when it comes to the work I hope to do, he destroys me. He says: "My wife is a dreamer." If wanting to be what I am is dreaming, then I want to be a dreamer.'

35

The woman looked out at the terrace. School satchel in hand, stamping the snow off his boots, the child appeared. He came in by the terrace door and laughed. The woman asked why he was laughing.

The child: 'I've never seen you in glasses before.'

The woman took her glasses off and put them on again. 'You're back so early.'

The child: 'They dropped two classes again.'

While the woman went on typing, the child came closer and sat down; he was very quiet. The woman stopped working and looked into space. 'You're hungry, aren't you?' she said. The child shook his head.

The woman: 'Do you mind my doing this?'

The child smiled to himself.

Later she worked in the bedroom, at a table by the window. The child appeared in the doorway with his fat friend. 'It's so cold out,' he said. 'And we can't go to Jürgen's house, because they're cleaning.'

The woman: 'But they were cleaning yesterday.' The child shrugged, and she turned back to her work.

The children stayed in the doorway. Though they didn't move, the woman was conscious of their presence and turned round.

Later, while she was writing, the sound of a record came from the next room: the screeching voices of actors imitating children and goblins. She stood up and went down the hallway to the room. The record

36

was turning on a small record player; there was no one to be seen. She turned it off, and in the same moment the children rushed screaming from behind the curtains, apparently to frighten her; since they had also exchanged clothes, they succeeded.

She said to them, 'Look. What I'm doing is work, even if it doesn't look that way to you. A little peace and quiet means a lot to me. When I'm working, I can't think of other things; it's not like when I'm cooking, for instance.'

The children gazed at the air and began, first one, then the other, to grin.

The woman: 'Won't you try to understand?'

The child: 'Are you cooking something for us now?'

The woman bowed her head. Then the child said malignantly, 'I'm sad too. You're not the only one.'

She sat at the typewriter, in the bedroom; she didn't type. It was quiet in the house. The children came in from the hallway, whispering and giggling. Suddenly the woman pushed the typewriter aside, and it fell to the floor.

In a hypermarket in the vicinity she loaded enormous packages into a large trolley and pushed it from section to section of the enormous store until it was full. At the checkout she stood in a long queue; the trolleys of those ahead of her were just as full as hers. In the car park she pushed the heavy cart, whose wheels kept turning to one side, to her car. She loaded the car, even the back seat; she couldn't see out of the rear window. At home she stored her purchases in the cellar, because all the cupboards and the deep freezer were already full.

At night she sat at the table in the living room. She put a sheet of paper into the typewriter and sat still, looking at it. After a while she folded her arms over the typewriter and laid her head on her arms.

Later in the night she was still there in the same position, now asleep.

She awoke, switched off the lamp, and left the room. Her face showed the pattern of the sleeve of her jumper. The only lights still on in the estate were the street lamps.

They visited Bruno at his office in the city. From the window one could see the city skyline. Bruno sat with her on a sofa, while the child read at a table in the corner.

He looked at the child. 'Franziska thinks Stefan has been strikingly withdrawn lately. She also says that he doesn't wash any more. In her opinion those are indications ... '

The woman: 'And what else does Franziska think?'

Bruno laughed; the woman smiled. When he held out his hand to her, she started back. He only said, 'Marianne.'

The woman: 'I'm sorry.'

Bruno: 'I was only trying to get a look at your coat; there's a button missing.'

They fell into a hopeless silence.

Bruno said to the child, 'Stefan, I'm going to show you how I intimidate people who come to my office.' He took the woman by the arm, and using her as a foil, acted out the following scene, with now and then a look of connivance at the child: 'First I make my victim sit in a corner, where he feels helpless. When I speak, I thrust my face right into his. If my caller is an elderly person' – his voice fell to a whisper – 'I speak very softly to make him think his hearing has suddenly failed him. It's also important to wear a certain kind of shoes, with crêpe soles, like these that I'm wearing; they're power shoes. And they have to be polished until they glow. One has to emanate an aura of mystery. But the main thing is the intimidating face.' He sat down facing the woman and began to stare; supporting his elbow on the table and holding up his forearm, he closed his fingers to make a fist, but not entirely: his thumb still protruded, as though prepared to thrust and gouge. While staring, he twisted his lips into a grimace, and said, 'I've also got a special salve from America; I put it around my eyes to stop me from blinking, or around my mouth to keep my lips from twitching.' Then and there he smeared salve around his eyes. 'This is my power stare, with the help of which I hope to become a member of the board soon.' He stared, and the woman and child looked at him.

He waved his hand to show that the act was over and said to the child, 'Next Sunday we'll go to the greenhouse at the Botanical Gardens and see the carnivorous plants. Or to the Planetarium. They project the Southern Cross on a dome that looks like the night sky – it's as if you were really in the South Seas.'

He took them to the door. He whispered something in the woman's ear; she looked at him and shook her head. After a pause, Bruno said, 'Nothing is settled, Marianne,' and let her out.

Alone, he hammered his face with his fist.

The woman and the child left the office building. Stepping out into the quiet street, they shut their eyes, dazzled by the glare of the winter afternoon. They turned onto a busy street with bank buildings on both sides, one reflected in the windows of another, and walked towards the city centre. At some traffic lights the child assumed the attitudes of the little men on the signals, first in stopping, then in crossing. In the pedestrian precinct he kept stopping at shop windows; the woman went ahead, then stopped to wait. In the end she always came back to pull the child along. Every few steps there was a poster advertising the evening edition of a mass-circulation newspaper, always with the same headlines. As the sky began to darken, they crossed a bridge over a river. The traffic was heavy. The child was talking. The woman gestured that she couldn't hear him, and the child shrugged. They walked along the river in the dusk, the child moving in a different rhythm from hers, first stopping, then running, so that she was always having to wait or run after him. For a while she walked beside the child, exaggerating the briskness of her stride as an example, prodding him with silent gestures. When he stopped to stare at a bush some distance away, hardly visible in the twilight, she stamped her foot and the heel of her shoe broke off. Two young men passed close to her and belched in her face. The woman and the child stopped at a public lavatory by the river. She had to take the child into the men's side, because he was afraid to go in alone. They locked themselves into a cubicle; the woman closed her eyes and leaned her back against the door. Above the partition separating their cubicle from the next a man's head appeared; he had jumped up from the floor. A second later it appeared again. Then the man's grinning face appeared below the partition, at her broken shoe. They passed a ground-floor flat where the television was on. An enormous bird flew across the foreground of the screen. An old woman fell on her face in the middle of the street. Two men whose cars had collided sprang at each other; one tried to strike out, but the other held him motionless.

It was almost night. The woman and the child were in the centre of the city, at a snack bar between two big office buildings, and the child was eating a pretzel. The roar of the traffic was so loud that a long-lasting catastrophe seemed to be in progress. A man came into the snack bar; he was bent almost double and had his hand on his heart. He asked for a glass of water and gulped it down with a pill. Then he sat down, stooped and wretched. The evening church bells rang, a fire engine passed, followed by a number of ambulances with blue lights and sirens. The light flashed over the woman's face; her forehead was beaded with perspiration, her lips cracked and parched.

Late in the evening she stood by the long windowless side wall of the living room, in the half shadow of the desk lamp: deep quiet; dogs barking in the distance.

Then the phone. She let it ring a few times, then answered in a soft voice. The publisher said in French that her voice sounded strange.

The woman: 'Maybe it's because I've been working. That seems to affect my voice.'

The publisher: 'Are you alone?'

The woman: 'The child is with me, as usual. He's asleep.'

The publisher: 'I'm alone too. It's a clear night. I can see the hills where you live.'

The woman: 'I'd love to see you in the daytime.'

The publisher: 'Are you working hard, Marianne? Or do you just sit around, out there in your wilderness?'

The woman: 'I was in town with Stefan today. He doesn't understand me. He thinks the big buildings, the petrol stations, the underground stations, and all that are wonderful.'

The publisher: 'Maybe there really is a new beauty that we just haven't learned to see. I love the city myself. From the roof of our building I can see as far as the airport; I can see planes landing and taking off in the distance, without hearing them. There's a delicate beauty about it that moves me deeply.' And after a pause, 'And what are you going to do now?'

The woman: 'Put on my nicest dress.'

The publisher: 'You mean we can get together?'

The woman: 'I'm going to dress to go on working.

All of a sudden I feel like it.'

The publisher: 'Do you take pills?'

The woman: 'Now and then – to keep awake.'

The publisher: 'I'd better not say anything, because I know you take every warning as a threat. Just try not to get that sad, resigned look that so many of my translators have.'

She let him ring off first; then she took a long silk dress from the closet. At the mirror she tried on a string of pearls but took them off again straight away. She stood silent, looking at herself from one side.

The grey of dawn lay over the estate; the street lamps had just gone out. The woman sat motionless at the desk.

She got up and, closing her eyes, zigzagged about the room; then she paced back and forth, turning on her heel every time she came to a wall. Then she walked backwards very quickly, turning aside and again turning aside. In the kitchen she stood at the sink, which was piled high with dirty dishes. She put the dishes into the dishwasher and reached over to the counter and turned on the transistor, which instantly began to blare wake-up music and cheery speaking voices. She turned it off, bent down, and opened the washing machine; she took out a tangled

44

wad of wet sheets and dropped them on the kitchen floor. She scratched her forehead violently until it bled.

She opened the letter-box outside the house; it was full of printed circulars. No handwriting except perhaps for the imitation script on the personalised advertising letters. She crumpled the sheaf of papers and tore them up. She went about the bungalow, putting it in order, stopping, turning around, bending down, scraping at a spot here and there in passing, picking up a single grain of rice and taking it to the rubbish bin in the kitchen. She sat down, stood up, took a few steps, sat down again. She took a roll of paper towels that was leaning in a corner, unrolled it, rolled it up again, and finally put it down not far from its old place.

The child sat watching as she moved fitfully around him. With a brush she swept the chair he was sitting on and silently motioned him to stand up. No sooner had he done so than she pushed him away with her elbow and brushed the seat of his chair, which was not the least bit dirty. The child moved back a step or two and stood still. Suddenly she flung the brush at him with all her might, but only hit a glass on the table, which shattered. She came at the child with clenched fists, but he only looked at her.

The doorbell rang; they both wanted to answer. She gave the child a push and he fell backwards.

When she opened the door, no one seemed to be there. Then she looked down, and there was the child's fat friend, crouching, he had a crooked grin on his face.

She sat rigid in the living room while the child and his fat friend jumped from a chair onto a pile of pillows, singing at the top of their voices: 'The shit jumps on the piss, and the piss jumps on the shit, and the shit jumps on the spit ... ' They screeched and writhed with laughter, whispered into each other's ears, looked at the woman, pointed at her, and laughed some more. They didn't stop and they didn't stop; the woman did not react.

She sat at the typewriter. The child came up on tiptoes and leaned against her. She pushed him away with her shoulder, but he kept standing beside her. Suddenly the woman pulled him close and grabbed him by the throat; she shook him, let him go, and averted her eyes.

At night the woman sat at the desk; something rose slowly from the lower edge of her eyes and made them glisten; she was crying, without a sound, without a movement.

In the daylight she walked along a straight road, in the midst of a flat, treeless, frozen landscape. On and on she walked, always straight ahead. She was still walking when night fell.

*

She sat in the local cinema with the two children beside her, surrounded by th cataclysmic din of an animated cartoon. Her eyes closed, she dozed off, then shook herself awake. Her head drooped on Stefan's shoulder. Open-mouthed, the child kept his eyes on the picture. She slept on the child's shoulder until the end of the film.

That night she stood over the typewriter and read aloud what she had written. '"'And no one helps you?' the visitor asked. 'No,' she replied. 'The man I dream of is the man who will love me for being the kind of woman who is not dependent on him.' 'And what will you love him for?' 'For that kind of love.'"' Once again she shrugged.

She lay in bed with her eyes open. On the bedside table beside her there was a glass of water and a clasp knife. Outside, someone hammered on the shutters and shouted something. She unclasped the knife, got up, and put on her dressing-gown. The voice was Bruno's. 'Open or I'll kick the door in. Let me in or I'll blow the house up.' She put the knife down, switched on the light, opened the terrace door, and let Bruno in. His coat was open over his shirt.

They stood facing each other; they passed through the hallway to the living room, where the light was on. Again they stood facing each other.

Bruno: 'You leave the light on at night.' He looked around. 'You've moved the furniture, too.' He picked up some books. 'And now you've got entirely different books.' He stepped closer to her. 'And the make-up case I brought you from the Far East – I bet you haven't got it any more.'

The woman: 'Won't you take your coat off? Would you care for a glass of vodka?'

Bruno: 'You're being pretty formal aren't you?' And after a pause, 'How about yourself? Haven't you got cancer yet?'

The woman didn't answer.

Bruno: 'Is one permitted to smoke?'

He sat down, she remained standing.

Bruno: 'So here you are, living the good life, alone with *your* son, in a nice warm house with garden and garage and good fresh air! Let's see, how old are you? You'll soon have folds in your neck and hairs growing out of your moles. Little spindly legs with a potato sack on top of them. You'll get older and older, you'll say you don't mind, and one day you'll hang yourself. You'll stink in your grave as uncouthly as you've lived. And how do you pass the time in the meanwhile? You probably sit around biting your nails. Right?'

The woman: 'Don't shout. The child is asleep.'

Bruno: 'You say "the child" as if I'd forfeited the right to use his name. And you're always so reasonable. You women, with your infernal reason. With your ruthless understanding of everything and everyone. And you're never bored, you bitches. Nothing could suit you better than sitting around and letting the time pass. Do you know why you women can never amount to anything? Because you never get drunk by yourselves! You lounge around your tidy homes like narcissistic photos of yourselves. Always acting mysterious, squeaking to cover your emptiness, devoted comrades who stifle people with your stupid humanitarianism, machines for the emasculation of all life. You creep and crawl, sniffing the ground, until death wrenches your mouths open.' He spat to one side: 'You and your new life! I've never known a woman make a lasting change in her life. Nothing but escapades – then back to the same old story. You know what? When you remember what you're doing now, it will be like leafing through faded newspaper clippings. You'll think of it as the only event in your life. And at the same time you'll realise that you were only following the fashions. Marianne's winter fashion.'

The woman: 'You thought that out before you came, didn't you? You didn't come here to talk to me or be with me.'

Bruno shouted, 'I'd rather talk to a ghost.'

The woman: 'You look awfully sad, Bruno.'

Bruno: 'You only say that to disarm me.'

For a long time they said nothing. Then Bruno laughed; he turned away and sobbed for a moment, then pulled himself together. 'I walked here. I wanted to kill you.' The woman stepped closer, and he said, 'Don't touch me. Please don't touch me.' After a pause, 'Sometimes I think you're just experimenting with me, putting me to the test. That makes me feel a little better.' After another pause, 'Yesterday I caught myself thinking what a comfort it would be at times if there were a God.'

The woman looked at him and said, 'Why, you've shaved your beard off.'

Bruno shrugged. 'I did it a week ago. And you've got new curtains.'

The woman: 'Not at all. It's still the old ones. It would make Stefan happy to get a letter from you.'

Bruno nodded and the woman smiled.

He asked her why she was smiling.

'It just occurred to me that you're the first grown-up I've spoken to in days.'

After they had stood for quite some time, each making little gestures as though in private, Bruno asked how she was getting along.

The woman answered calmly, as though not speaking of herself at all, 'One gets so tired all alone in the house.'

She went with him when he left. They walked side by side as far as the phone box. Suddenly Bruno stopped walking and stretched out on the ground with his face down. She crouched beside him.

On a cold morning the woman sat in a rocking chair on the terrace, but she wasn't rocking. The child stood beside her, watching the clouds of vapour that came out of his mouth. The woman looked into the distance; the pines were reflected in the window behind her.

In the evening she walked through the almost empty streets of the small town, as if she were going somewhere. She stopped in front of a large, lighted ground-floor window. A group of women were sitting in a kind of school-room with a blackboard. Franziska was standing at the blackboard with a piece of chalk, inaudibly elucidating some economic principle. Notebooks were clapped shut; Franziska sat down with the others. She said something that made the others laugh, not aloud, more to themselves. Two women had their arms around each other. Another woman was smoking a pipe. Still another was wiping something off her neighbour's cheek. Franziska stopped talking, and a few women raised their hands. Franziska counted the hands, then some

51

others raised theirs. In the end they all banged their desks as though in applause. The scene seemed peaceful, as though these women were not a group but individuals brought together by an inner need.

The woman left the window. She walked through the deserted streets. The clock in the church tower struck. When she passed the church, people were singing inside and someone was playing the organ.

She went in and stood to one side. Several people were standing in the pews, led in song by the priest; now and then someone coughed. A child was sitting in the midst of the standing singers with his thumb in his mouth. The organ droned. After a while the woman left.

On the way back to the estate, along the dark avenue of trees, she made gestures as though talking to herself.

During the night she got up, stood alone in the kitchen, and drank a glass of water. Then there was a stillness, with no other sound than the beating of her heart.

At midday the woman and Franziska, both bundled up, sat side by side on the terrace, in two rocking chairs. They watched the children, who were chopping up the dried-out Christmas tree and throwing the pieces into a fire.

After a while Franziska said, 'I understand why you couldn't come in to our meeting. I, too, have moments, especially just before I have to leave my quiet apartment for a meeting, when the thought of going out among people suddenly makes me feel dead tired ... '

The woman: 'I'm waiting for your "but".'

Franziska: 'I used to be the same as you. One day, for instance, I couldn't speak. I wrote what I had to say on slips of paper. Or I'd open the wardrobe door and stand there for hours weeping, because I couldn't decide what to put on. Once I was on my way somewhere with a man, and suddenly I couldn't take another step. He pleaded with me and I just stood there. Of course I was a lot younger ... Haven't you any desire to be happy, in the company of others?'

The woman: 'No. I don't want to be happy. At the most, contented. I'm afraid of happiness. I don't think I could bear it, here in my head. I'd go mad for good, or die. Or I'd murder someone.'

Franziska: 'You mean you want to be alone like this all your life? Don't you long for someone who would be your friend, body and soul?'

The woman cried out, 'Oh yes. I do. But I don't want to know who he is. Even if I were always with him, I wouldn't want to know him. There's just one thing I'd like' – she smiled, apparently at herself – 'I'd like him to be clumsy, a real butterfingers. I honestly

53

don't know why.' She interrupted herself. 'Oh, Franziska, I'm talking like a teenager.'

Franziska: 'I have an explanation for the butterfingers. Isn't your father like that? The last time he was here he wanted to shake hands with me across the table and he stuck his fingers in the mustard pot instead.'

The woman laughed and the child turned his head, as though it were unusual for his mother to laugh.

Franziska: 'By the way, he's arriving on the afternoon train. I wired him to come. He's expecting you to meet him at the station.'

After a pause the woman said, 'You shouldn't have done that. I don't want anyone just now. Everything seems so banal with people around.'

Franziska: 'I believe you're beginning to regard people as nothing more than unfamiliar sounds in the house.' She put her hand on the woman's arm.

The woman said, 'In the book I've been translating there's a quotation from Baudelaire; he says the only political action he understands is revolt. Suddenly it flashed through my mind that the only political action I could understand would be to run amok.'

Franziska: 'As a rule, only men do that.'

The woman: 'By the way, how are you getting along with Bruno?'

Franziska: 'Bruno seems made for happiness. That's why he's so lost now. And so theatrical! He's getting on my nerves. I'm going to throw him out.'

The woman: 'Oh, Franziska. You always say that. When you're always the one that gets left.'

After two or three attempts to protest, Franziska said with a note of surprise, 'To tell the truth, you're right.'

They looked at each other. The children seemed to have fallen out; they stood with their backs to each other gazing at the air, the fat one rather sadly. The woman called out, 'Hey, children, no quarrels today.'

The fat boy smiled with relief and – circuitously, to be sure, and with downcast eyes – the two of them moved closer to each other.

The woman and the child were waiting at the local station. The train pulled in and the woman's father, a pale old man in glasses, waved from behind a window. Years ago he had been a successful writer, and now he sent carbon copies of short sketches to the papers. He couldn't get the door open; the woman opened it from outside and helped him down to the platform. They looked at each other and in the end they were pleased. The father shrugged, looked in different directions, wiped his lips, and said his hands smelled unpleasant from the metal of the train.

At home he sat on the floor with the child, who took

his presents out of his grandfather's bag: a compass and a set of dice. The child pointed at various objects in the house and outside and asked what colour they were. Many of the old man's answers were wrong.

The child: 'So you're still colour-blind?'

The grandfather: 'It's just that I never learned to see colours.'

The woman came in, carrying light-blue tea things on a silver tray. The tea steamed as she poured it, and her father warmed his hands on the pot. While he was sitting on the floor, an assortment of coins and a bunch of keys had fallen out of his pocket. The woman picked them up. 'Your pockets are full of loose change again,' she said.

The father: 'That purse you gave me, it didn't last long. I lost it on the way home.'

Over tea, he said, 'The other day I was expecting a visitor. The moment I opened the door, I saw that he was drenched in rain from head to foot, and I'd just cleaned the house. While I was letting him in and shaking hands with him, I noticed that I was standing on the doormat wiping my feet for all I was worth, as if I were the wet visitor.' He giggled.

'And you felt caught in the act. Does that still happen to you so often?'

The father giggled and held his hand before his mouth. 'What will embarrass me most of all is lying on my deathbed with my mouth open.'

He swallowed some tea the wrong way.

Then the woman said, 'Tonight you'll sleep in Bruno's room, Father.'

The father replied, 'It doesn't matter. I'll be leaving tomorrow.'

That evening the woman was writing in the living room; her father was sitting at some distance from her, watching her over a bottle of wine. After a while he came closer, and she looked up, undisturbed. He bent over her. 'There's a button missing on your coat. I've just noticed it.' She took off her coat and handed it to him.

As she went on typing, he sewed on the button with needle and thread from a hotel sewing packet. Again his eyes rested on her. She noticed and gave him a questioning look. He apologised. And then he said, 'You've become so beautiful, Marianne!' She smiled.

She finished typing and made a few corrections. Her father tried in vain to open a fresh bottle of wine. She came to his assistance. He went to the kitchen to get her a glass. She called out to tell him where the glasses were. She heard him pottering for quite some time, then silence. In the end she went in and showed him.

They sat across from one another, drinking. The father made a futile gesture or two. The woman said,

'Go ahead and say it. That's what you came for, isn't it?'

The father gesticulated again and shook his head. 'Shall we go out for a while?' He pointed in various directions. Then he said, 'When you were a child, you never wanted to go walking with me. I had only to utter the word "walk" to turn you against it. But you were always ready for an "evening stroll".'

In the darkness they walked along the driveway, past the garages - the bonnets of some of the cars were still giving off crackling sounds. When they reached the phone box, the father said, 'I've got a quick phone call to make.'

The woman: 'You can phone from the house.'

The father replied simply, 'My companion is waiting.' And then he was in the box, a blurred, gesticulating figure behind the translucent glass.

They walked uphill past the sleeping bungalows. Once a lavatory flushed; there was no other sound.

The woman: 'What does your companion say?'

The father: 'She wanted to know if I had taken my pills.'

The woman: 'Is it the same one as last year?'

The father: 'This one lives in another city.'

They walked along the upper edge of the estate, where the forest began. Small snowflakes fell rustling through the withered oak leaves and collected on frozen puddles of dogs' urine.

The woman and her father stopped walking and looked down at the lights in the plain. In one of the box-like houses at their feet someone started playing the piano: *Für Elise.*

The woman asked, 'Are you happy, Father?'

The father shook his head. Then, as though a gesture were not sufficient answer, he said, 'No.'

'Have you some idea about how one might live?'

The father: 'Oh, stop it. Don't say such things.'

They started walking again, skirting the woods; now and then the woman leaned her head back and snowflakes fell on her face. She looked into the woods; the snow was falling so lightly that nothing moved. Far behind the thinly spaced trees there was a fountain; the thin stream of water that flowed into it tinkled as it fell.

The woman asked, 'Do you still write?'

The father laughed. 'You mean will I keep on writing till the day I die.' He turned towards her. 'I believe that at some time I began to live in the wrong direction – though I don't hold the war or any other outside event to blame. Now writing sometimes strikes me as a pretext' – he giggled – 'and then again sometimes it doesn't. I'm so alone that before I go to sleep at night I often have nobody to think about, simply because I haven't seen anyone during the day. And how can anyone write if they have no one to think about? On the other hand, I see this woman now and then, chiefly because if something happens to me I'd prefer to be found fairly soon and not lie around too long as a corpse.' He giggled.

The woman: 'That's enough of your silly jokes.'

The father pointed up at the forest: 'The mountain top is back there, but you can't see it from here.'

The woman: 'Do you ever cry?'

The father: 'I did once – a year ago, sitting at home one evening. And afterwards I wanted to go out.'

The woman: 'Does the time still hang as heavy on your hands as when you were young?'

The father: 'Oh, heavier than ever. Once every day it seems to stop altogether. Now, for instance. It's been dark for hours, and I keep having to remind myself the night is only beginning.'

He moved his hands around his head.

The woman imitated the gesture and asked him what it meant.

The father: 'I've just wound heavy cloths around my head at the thought of the long night.' This time he didn't giggle but openly laughed. 'You'll end up the same as me, Marianne. And with this observation my mission here is fulfilled.'

They smiled, and the woman said, 'Wouldn't you say it was getting cold?'

They went down the slope on the other side of the estate. Once the father stopped and raised his forefinger. The woman kept going but turned round to him and said, 'Don't keep stopping every time you get an idea, Father. Even when I was little, that used to get on my nerves.'

The next day they were walking through the women's clothing section of a large department store in a nearby shopping centre. A foreign woman came out of a dressing room, wearing a green suit. The salesgirl said to her, 'It looks just lovely on you.' The father stepped up and said, 'That simply isn't true. The suit is hideous and it's not at all becoming to her.' His daughter hurried up to him and pulled him away.

They rode on an escalator, and he stumbled at the top. As they walked along, he looked at her and said, 'We really must have our picture taken together. Is there a photo machine in this place?' When they found one, a man was busy changing the developer. The father bent over a strip of four sample photos displayed on the side of the booth: in them a young man bared his upper front teeth in a smile, and in one of the exposures there was a girl with him. The maintenance man closed the box and straightened up. The father looked at him, then pointed with an air of surprise at the photos and said, 'That's you, isn't it?'

The man stood beside his pictures: he had aged a

good deal since then; now he was almost bald and his smile was different. The father asked about the girl, but the man only made a gesture as of throwing something behind him, and went away.

After having their pictures taken, they roamed about, waiting for them to develop. When they came back the machine ejected a strip of photos. The woman reached for it, but the pictures were of a man, a total stranger.

She looked around. The man in the pictures stood behind her and said, 'Your pictures were ready long ago. I've taken the liberty of looking at them. I hope you'll forgive me.' They exchanged photos. The father took a good look at the man and said, 'You're an actor, aren't you?'

The man nodded silently and averted his eyes. 'But I'm unemployed at the moment.'

The father: 'I've seen you in films. You always seem to be embarrassed at the thought of what you have to say next. That's what makes it really awkward.'

The man laughed and again averted his eyes.

The father: 'Are you such a coward in private life, too?'

After laughing and averting his eyes yet again, the man met the father's gaze for a moment.

The father: 'Your trouble, I believe, is that you always hold back something of yourself. You're not shameless enough for an actor. You want to be a personality, like the actors in those American films, but you never risk your own self. As a result you're always posing.'

The man looked at the woman, but she didn't come to his rescue.

The father: 'In my opinion you should learn how to run properly and scream properly, with your mouth wide open. I've noticed that even when you yawn you're afraid to open your mouth all the way.' He poked the man in the stomach and the man doubled up. 'You haven't been keeping yourself in trim, either. How long have you been unemployed.'

The man: 'I've stopped counting the days.'

The father: 'In your next film make a sign to show that you've understood me.'

The man smacked the palm of his hand with his fist. The father made the same gesture. 'That's it!' He walked away, but called back. 'You haven't even been discovered yet. I'm looking forward to seeing you grow older from film to film.'

The actor and the woman looked after the old man; before going their ways they began to shake hands, but instantly recoiled from the slight electric shock.

The woman said, 'Everything's full of electricity in the winter.'

They separated, but then they found that they were going the same way and proceeded side by side in silence. At the car park they overtook the old man. They nodded goodbye but went on together when it turned out that their cars were almost next to each other.

On the road the woman saw the actor pass her; he was looking straight ahead. She turned into a side road.

The woman stood on the station platform with her father and the child. When the train pulled in, she said, 'It has done me good to have you here, Father.' She wanted to say something more but only stammered. Her father made various gestures, then suddenly said to the child, who had picked up the suitcases, 'You know that I still can't distinguish colours. But there's something else I want you to know: I'll soon be an old man, but I still don't wear carpet slippers around the house. I'm almost proud of it.' He hopped nimbly up the steps backwards and vanished inside the train, which was already in motion. The child said, 'He's not so clumsy after all.'

The woman: 'It's always been an act with him.'

They stood on the empty platform – the next train wasn't due for an hour – and looked at the gentle slope of the mountain behind the town. The woman said, 'Let's climb up there tomorrow. I've never been to the top.' The child nodded. 'But we can't dawdle.

The days are still very short. Bring your new compass.'

Late in the afternoon they were at a nearby open-air zoo. A good many people were moving silently through the grounds. A few were standing still and laughing in a hall of mirrors. The sun went down, and most of the visitors headed for the exit. The woman and child stood looking at one of the cages. It was getting dark and windy; they were almost alone. The child drove an electric car around a circular track, and the woman sat on a bench at the edge of the concrete surface.

She stood up and the child called out, 'It's so nice here. I don't want to go home yet.'

The woman: 'Neither do I. I only stood up because it's so nice.' She looked at the western sky, the lower edge of which was still yellow. Against it the leafless branches looked barer than usual. A sudden gust of wind drove some leaves across the concrete. They seemed to come from another season.

It was dark when they reached the bungalow. There was a letter in the letter-box. The woman recognised Bruno's handwriting on the envelope and gave the letter to the child. She put the key in the lock but didn't open the door. The child waited; then finally he asked, 'Aren't we going in?'

The woman: 'Let's stay out here a little while.'

They stood for quite some time. A man with an attaché case came along and kept looking round at them after he had passed.

That evening, while the woman cooked dinner, slipping into the living room now and then to correct her manuscript, the child read Bruno's letter to himself in an undertone: '"Dear Stefan, Yesterday I saw you on your way home from school. I couldn't very well stop because I was caught in a line of cars. You had a headlock on your fat friend."' At this point the reading child smiled. '"Sometimes it seems to me that you never existed. I want to see you soon and"' – here the reading child frowned – '"sniff you ... "'

During the night the woman sat alone in the living room and listened to music – the same record over and over again:

The Left-Handed Woman

She came with others out of the Underground.

She ate with others in a snack bar,
She sat with others in a Launderette,
But once I saw her alone, reading the papers
Posted on the wall of a news-stand.

She came with others out of an office building,
With others she jostled her way up to a
Market stall,
She sat with others on the edge of a playground,
But once I saw her through a window
Playing chess all alone.

She lay with others on a park lawn,
She laughed with others in a
Hall of mirrors,
She screamed with others on a roller coaster,
And after that the only time I saw her alone
Was walking through my wishful dreams.

But today in my open house:
The telephone receiver is facing the wrong way,
The pencil lies to the left of the writing pad,
The teacup next to it has its handle on the
Left,
The apple beside it has been peeled the wrong way
(but not completely),
The curtains have been thrown open from the left
And the key to the front door is in the left

Coat pocket.
Left-handed woman, you've given yourself away!
Or did you mean to give me a sign?

I want to see you in a foreign continent,
For there at last I shall see you alone among others,
And among a thousand others you will see me,
And at last we shall go to meet each other.

In the morning the woman and the child, not conspicuously dressed for the mountain, which was not very high, stepped out of the house. They walked past other bungalows, and once they stopped outside one of the almost windowless housefronts and looked at a brown door to the left and right of which two black-stemmed lanterns had been fixed, as though to decorate a gigantic sarcophagus.

On the gently rising forest path the sun was perceptible only as a sombre light. Turning off the path, they climbed a slope and passed a fishpond, which had been drained for the winter. Deep in the woods they stopped at a Jewish graveyard; the tombstones had sunk halfway into the ground. Farther up, the wind whistled on such a high note that it almost hurt their ears. Here the snow was pure white, while farther down there had been grains of soot on it, and here dog tracks gave way to deer tracks.

They climbed through underbrush. Birds were singing on every side. Fed by the melting snow, a little brook rushed loudly past. A few dry leaves stirred on the thin branches of the oak trees; strips of white bark hung trembling from the birch trunks.

They crossed a clearing, at the edge of which some deer stood huddled together. The snow was not very deep; stalks of withered grass peered out and bent in the wind.

The higher they climbed, the brighter grew the light. Their faces were scratched and sweaty. At the top – it hadn't been very far – they made a brush fire in the lee of a boulder.

In the early afternoon they sat by the fire and looked down into the plain, where now and then a car sent up a flash of sunlight; the child has his compass in his hand. Once, far below, a spot shone bright for a time and then vanished – a closed window among many open ones.

It was so cold that no sooner had the clouds of smoke rising from the fire left the shelter of the boulder than they dispersed into wisps and vanished. The woman and the child ate potatoes that they had brought along in a little sack and roasted in the coals, and drank hot coffee out of a thermos flask. The woman turned to the child, who was sitting motionless, looking down into the plain. She stroked his back lightly, and he laughed, as though that were the most plausible thing to do.

After a while she said, 'Once you sat by the sea like this, looking at the waves for hours. Do you remember?'

The child: 'Of course I remember. It was getting dark, but I didn't want to go. You and Bruno were angry because you wanted to go back to the hotel. You were wearing a green skirt and a white blouse with lace cuffs, and a wide hat that you had to hold on to because the wind was blowing. There weren't any shells on that beach, only round stones.'

The woman: 'When you start remembering, I'm always afraid you'll confound me with something I did long ago.'

The child: 'Next day Bruno pushed you into the water with your clothes on as a joke. You were wearing brown shoes that fastened with a button...'

The woman: 'But do you also remember the evening when you lay motionless on your back in the sandbox outside the house and didn't stir a muscle?'

The child: 'I don't know anything about that.'

The woman said, 'Then it's my turn to remember. Your head was resting on your hands and one leg was bent at the knee. It was summer, a clear moonless night; the sky was full of stars. You lay on your back in the sand and no one dared say a word to you.'

70

After a time the child said, 'Maybe because it was so quiet in the sandbox.'

They looked down into the plain, ate and drank. Abruptly the woman laughed and shook her head. Then she told him a story. 'Years ago I saw some pictures by an American painter. There were fourteen of them. They were supposed to be the Stations of the Cross – you know, Jesus sweating blood on the Mount of Olives, being scourged, and so on. But these paintings were only black-and-white shapes – a white background and criss-crossing black stripes. The next-to-last station – where Jesus is taken down from the cross – was almost all black, and the last one, where Jesus is laid in the tomb, was all white. And now the strange part of it: I passed slowly in front of the pictures, and when I stopped to look at the last one, the one that was all white, I suddenly saw a wavering after-image of the almost black one; it lasted only a few moments and then there was only the white.'

The child tried to whistle but couldn't manage it in the cold. The woman said, 'Let's take a picture before we go.'

The child photographed her with an ungainly old Polaroid camera. The picture showed her very much from below, looking down; behind her there was only sky and the barest suggestion of treetops. The woman pretended to be horrified. 'So that's how grown-ups look to children!'

At home she got into the bath and the child got in with her. They both leaned back and closed their eyes. The child said, 'I can still see the trees on the mountain.' Steam rose from the water. The child whistled in the bath and the woman looked at him almost severely.

Later she sat up straight at the typewriter and typed rapidly. In the twilight the estate looked as though it belonged to the forest, which rose up behind it, and to the darkening sky.

In the morning the woman, among others, walked about the pedestrian precinct of the small town; she was carrying a rumpled, tired-looking plastic bag. One of the people up ahead of her was Bruno. She followed him. After a while he turned round as though by chance, and instantly she said, 'The other day I saw a sweater that would be just right for you in that shop.' She took his arm and they went in. A salesgirl was sitting, resting, with a mannequin behind her. Her eyes were closed and her hands, which were somewhat red and rough, lay in her lap; her brows were drawn together as though relaxation were painful, and the corners of her mouth drooped. She jumped up as they came in, upsetting her chair and stumbling over a clothes hanger that was lying on the floor.

She sneezed, put on her glasses, sneezed again.

The woman said slowly, as though to soothe her, 'Last week, I saw a man's sweater in the window. Grey cashmere.'

The salesgirl fingered through a pile on one of the shelves. The woman, who was looking over the salesgirl's shoulder, picked out the sweater and handed it to Bruno to try on. A baby's scream could be heard from one corner of the shop, where there was a basket on the floor. The salesgirl said, 'I don't dare go near it with my cold.' The woman went over and pacified the child just by bending over the basket. Bruno had the sweater on; he looked at the salesgirl, who merely shrugged and gave her nose a prolonged blowing. The woman told Bruno in an undertone to keep it on. He was going to pay, but she shook her head, pointed at herself, and gave the salesgirl a banknote. The salesgirl pointed at the empty till, and the woman said in the same undertone that she would come by for the change next day. 'Or come and see me. Yes, come and see me.' She quickly wrote down the address. 'You're all alone with the baby, aren't you? It's nice to see someone in a shop who isn't a ghost with make-up on. Forgive me for talking about you as if I had a right to.'

As they were leaving, the salesgirl took out a pocket mirror and looked at herself; she held a chapstick under her nose and passed it over her lips.

Outside the woman said to Bruno, 'So you're still in the land of the living.'

Bruno answered almost gaily, 'I myself am surprised some afternoons to see that I'm still in existence. Yesterday, incidentally, I noticed that I've stopped counting the days since I've been without you.' He laughed. 'I had a dream in which people all went crazy, one after another. Every time it hit somebody, you could see that he began to enjoy his life, so there was no need for the rest of us to feel guilty. Does Stefan still ask for me?'

While removing the price tag from the back of the sweater, the woman said, 'Come soon.' She walked away, and he took another direction.

In the evening the woman was sitting in the café, reading a newspaper and muttering to herself. The actor came along and stopped at her table. 'I recognised your car in the car park,' he said.

She looked at him without surprise and said, 'I've been reading the paper again for the first time in ages. I'd lost track of what was going on in the world. What month is it anyway?'

The actor sat down across the table from her. 'February.'

'And what continent are we living on?'

'On one among several.'

The woman: 'Have you a name?'

The actor said it; he looked to one side, laughed, and moved the glasses around on the table. Finally he looked at her again and said, 'I've never followed a woman before. I've been looking for you for days. Your face is so gentle – as though you never forgot that we're all going to die. Forgive me if I've said something stupid.' He shook his head. 'Damn it, the second I say something I want to take it back! I've longed for you so these last few days that I couldn't keep still. Please don't be angry. You seem so free, you have a kind of' – he laughed – 'of lifeline in your face! I burn for you, everything in me is aflame with desire for you. Perhaps you think I'm overwrought from being out of work so long? But don't speak. You must come with me. Don't leave me alone. I want you. Don't you feel that we've been lost up to now? At a tram stop I saw these words on a wall: "HE loves you. HE will save you." Instantly I thought of you. HE won't save us: no, WE will save each other. I want to be all around you, sense your presence everywhere; I want my hand to feel the warmth rising from you even before I touch you. Don't laugh. Oh, how I desire you. I want to be with you right this minute, entirely and forever!'

They sat motionless, face to face. He looked almost angry; then he ran out of the café. The woman sat among the other people, without moving.

A brighly lighted bus came driving through the night, empty except for a few old women, passed slowly round a traffic roundabout, then vanished into the darkness, its strap handles swaying.

Another evening the woman and child sat in the living room, throwing dice. It was stormy outside and the doors rattled. Now and then the two of them stopped playing and listened to the roaring of the storm.

The phone rang. They let it ring for quite some time. Finally the child answered and said, 'I don't want to talk now.' Then to the woman, 'Bruno wants to come over with the teacher.' The woman made a gesture of assent, and the child said into the phone, 'Yes, I'll still be awake.'

As they went on playing, another bell rang. This time it was the door.

The publisher was outside. The instant the child opened the door, the publisher said, 'What is little, has tired eyes, and isn't in bed, though it's long after the children's programmes are over?'

He entered with long strides and embraced the woman.

She asked, 'Have you been to see your lost author again?'

The publisher: 'There is no lost author. Never has been.'

He pulled a bottle of champagne out of his coat pocket and said there was more in the car.

The woman: 'But do ask the chauffeur in.'

After a brief pause the publisher opened the door and beckoned to the chauffeur, who entered hesitantly, after wiping his shoes at great length.

The publisher: 'You are invited to share a glass with us.'

The woman: 'Or two.'

The doorbell rang again. When the chauffeur answered it, the salesgirl from the shop stood there smiling. She was beautiful now.

They all sat or stood drinking in the living room. The child went on throwing dice. Music. The publisher had his eyes on the floor; then he looked from one person to another. Suddenly he seemed pleased and refilled the chauffeur's glass.

Then it was the telephone ringing again. The woman answered and said at once, 'Yes, of course I know. Your voice sounds so close. You're in the phone box at the corner, I can tell.'

The doorbell rang, the short ring of a familiar.

The woman nodded to the others to get the door, while she stayed on the phone. 'No, I'm not alone. Can't you hear? But come ahead. Do come!'

Bruno and Franziska appeared.

Franziska said to the woman, 'And we were expecting to find the loneliest woman on earth.'

'I apologise for not being alone this evening. It's quite accidental.'

Franziska to the child: 'I have a name. So stop referring to me as "the teacher", the way you did on the telephone just now.'

The publisher: 'In that case, I don't want to be called "the publisher" any more, either; my name is Ernst.'

The woman embraced Bruno.

The publisher stepped up to Franziska and said, 'Let's you and me embrace, too' and his arms were already around her. The woman opened the door and went outside; the actor was coming slowly down the street. She let him in without a word.

Bruno looked him over. Then he said, 'Are you the boyfriend?' And then, 'I suppose you're sleeping with my wife. Or aiming to, at least?'

He stared as he had at the office. 'I bet you're the type that drives an ancient small car with a lot of political pornography magazines lying around on the back seat?'

He went on staring. 'Your shoes aren't shined either. But at least you're blond. Could it be that you have blue eyes?' After staring a little more he suddenly relaxed; the woman just stood there.

He said, 'I'm only talking, you know. It doesn't mean a thing.'

They were all in the living room. The publisher danced with the salesgirl. The chauffeur went out to the car and brought back some more bottles of champagne. Then he passed from one guest to another, clinking glasses.

The child was playing on the floor among them. Bruno squatted down and watched him.

The child: 'Will you play with me?'

Bruno: 'I can't play this evening.' He tossed the dice two or three times and said, 'Really, I can't play this evening.'

The salesgirl detached herself from the publisher, bent down, and threw the dice. Then she went on dancing, breaking away now and then to play dice with the child.

Filled glasses in hand, the publisher and Franziska walked around each other in circles.

Bruno cut the child's toenails in the bathroom.

The publisher and Franziska smiled as they slowly passed each other in the hallway.

The child lay in bed and Bruno stood beside him. The child said, 'You're all so strangely quiet.' Bruno only tilted his head to one side. Then he switched off the light.

He passed down the hallway with the woman to join the others. The actor came towards them; Bruno put his arm around his wife's shoulders, then took it away.

The actor said to her, 'I've been looking for you.'

They all sat in the living room, not talking very much. But without being asked they moved closer and closer together and stayed that way for a time.

The salesgirl leaned her head back and said, 'What a long day it's been. My eyes weren't eyes any more; they felt like burning holes. They don't hurt as much now and I'm gradually beginning to see again.'

The chauffeur, beside her, made a move as though to take hold of her hair, then let his hand drop.

The publisher knelt down in front of the salesgirl and kissed her fingertips, each separately.

The chauffeur took some photographs out of his wallet and showed them to each of the others in turn.

Franziska said to the salesgirl, 'Why don't you join a political party?'

The salesgirl made no reply but suddenly threw her arms around Franziska; Franziska disengaged herself, looked towards the woman, and said, 'Loneliness is a source of loathsome ice-cold suffering, the suffering of unreality. At such times we need people to teach us that we're not really so far gone.'

The chauffeur nodded energetically and looked at the publisher, who raised his arms and said, 'I haven't expressed any disagreement.'

The salesgirl hummed along with the music; then she lay down on the floor and stretched her legs.

The chauffeur took out a memo pad and started sketching them all.

Franziska began to open her mouth, but the chauffeur said, 'Please don't move.' Franziska closed her mouth again.

They were all silent; they drank; then more silence.

Suddenly they all laughed at once.

Bruno said to the actor: 'Do you realise that you're sitting in my place?'

The actor stood up and was going to take another chair. The sketching chauffeur said severely, 'Stay where you are!'

As the actor was sitting down again, Bruno pulled the chair out from under him and he fell on his back.

He got up slowly and took a kick at Bruno.

The two of them rolled on the floor; the chauffeur tried to separate them.

The salesgirl put her glasses on.

Franziska exchanged glances with the publisher, who launched into the story of how he had been shipwrecked during the war.

The woman looked out of the window; the crowns of the trees in the garden were being buffeted to and fro.

The chauffeur came back from the car with a first-aid kit.

He joined the hands of Bruno and the actor, stepped back, told them to stay in that exact position, and sketched. They made faces, and he cried out, 'Don't laugh!'

Bruno and the actor went to the bathroom and washed their faces together.

The salesgirl and Franziska came in and dabbed at them with towels.

The chauffeur showed his finished sketch around.

The woman and Bruno stood on the terrace. After a while Bruno asked, 'Have you decided what you're going to do with yourself?'

The woman answered, 'No. For a moment I saw my future clearly and it chilled me to the bone.'

They stood looking down at the garages; plastic bags were skittering over the pavement. The elderly woman was walking down the street without her dog, a long evening dress showing under her coat. She waved at them with both arms, as if she knew everything, and the two of them waved back.

The woman asked if he had to go to the office next day.

Bruno: 'Don't talk about it now.'

Arm-in-arm, they stepped through the terrace door into the living room. The chauffeur, who was drinking, pointed at them and cried out, 'By God, love still exists!'

The salesgirl slapped his outstretched finger and said, 'The child is sleeping.'

The chauffeur repeated his remark more softly.

The publisher, who was leaning against Franziska's chair, nodded and dozed off. Franziska stood up gingerly, took the chauffeur by the hand and danced with him, cheek to cheek.

The woman was standing by the window. The actor came over to her.

They both looked out; the stormy sky glittered with stars and was reflected in the space behind the stars. After a time he said, 'There are some galaxies so distant that their light is weaker than the mere background glow of the night sky. I would like to be somewhere with you now.'

The woman answered instantly, 'Please don't include me in any of your plans.'

The actor looked at her until she looked back at him. Suddenly she said, 'Once when I was in hospital I saw an old, sick, desperately sad woman caressing the nurse who was standing by her bed – but only her thumbnail. Over and over again, only her thumbnail.'

They went on looking at each other.

Finally the actor said, 'While we were looking at each other a moment ago, I saw the difficulties that have beset my life up to now as barriers that threatened my devotion to you, one barrier after another, and at the same time, as I continued to look at you, I felt that the difficulties were vanishing, one after another, until only you remained. I love you now. I love you.'

Bruno sat motionless, just drinking.

Taking over from the chauffeur, the salesgirl danced with Franziska.

Staggering a little, the chauffeur attempted a few steps towards this one and that one; in the end he stood still, all by himself.

Bruno versified into the air:

'Suffering's like a propeller
Except that it doesn't take you anywhere,
Whereas the propeller pulls you through the air.'

Franziska who was still dancing, heard him and laughed.

The actor looked around from the window at Bruno, who asked him if it wasn't a beautiful poem.

The publisher answered with his eyes closed, as though he had only been pretending to be asleep. 'I'll take it for our next year's house calendar.' He looked at the chauffeur. 'Hey, you're drunk.' With a single movement he stood up and said to Franziska, 'I'll drive you home. Where do you live?'

The chauffeur: 'Oh, let's stay a little longer. Tomorrow you won't speak to me anyway.'

The publisher, to Franziska: 'Haven't I met you somewhere?'

The salesgirl joined the woman at the window and said, 'In my attic I often stand under the skylight, just to look at the clouds. It makes me feel I'm still alive.'

The salesgirl looked at her watch, and immediately the woman turned to the publisher, who was dancing slowly past with Franziska. 'She has to go home to her child,' the woman said.

The publisher faced Franziska with his hand under his heart and bowed to the salesgirl. To the woman he said very seriously, 'So once again we have not seen each other by daylight.'

The publisher and the salesgirl went to the door; jingling the car keys, the chauffeur stumbled after them. The publisher took the keys.

When the woman shut the door behind them and came back into the room, Franziska was sitting there alone, tugging her short blonde hair. The woman looked around for Bruno and the actor, and Franziska indicated with a gesture that they were down in the cellar. The music had stopped and the sound of a ping-pong ball could be heard. Franziska and the woman sat facing each other; on the terrace the wind rocked the rocking chairs.

Franziska: 'The salesgirl and her baby! And you and your child! And tomorrow's another school day! To tell you the truth, children depress me. Sometimes I can tell by looking at them that they want to kill me with their voices, with their movements. They all shout at once. They rush back and forth until I'm sick with dizziness and ready to suffocate. What use are they? What do they give us?'

The woman hung her head as though in assent.

After a while she replied, 'Possibly a little more to think about.'

Franziska was holding a visiting card in her hand. 'As he was leaving, your publisher gave me his card.' She stood up. 'Now even I would like to be alone.'

The woman put her arm around her.

Franziska: 'Ah, that's better.'

At the open door, with her coat on, she said, 'I have my spies. They tell me you've been talking to yourself.'

The woman: 'I know. And I've come to like these little conversations so much that I exaggerate them on purpose.'

Franziska, after a pause: 'Close the door or you'll catch cold.' She walked slowly down the street, step after step, her head bent forward; one hand hung down behind as if she were pulling a loaded supermarket trolley after her.

The woman went down to the cellar, where Bruno and the actor were. Bruno asked, 'Are we the last?'

The woman nodded.

Bruno: 'We'll just finish this set.'

They played very earnestly. Folding her arms against the chill in the room, the woman watched them.

All three together, they mounted the stairs.

At the coat-rack, Bruno dressed to go out. So did the actor; at first he tried to put his head through one of the armholes of his sleeveless sweater.

The woman noticed and smiled.

She opened the door.

Bruno already had his coat on; the actor followed him out and said to Bruno, 'I've got my car.'

Bruno looked into space for a moment and then replied, 'That's good. I've perspired a bit.'

Standing at the door, the woman looked after them as they walked to the car.

They stopped and pissed side by side, with their backs to her. When they proceeded on their way, they kept changing sides, because neither wanted to be on the right.

The woman went back into the house. She closed the door and locked it. She carried glasses and bottles into the kitchen, emptied the ashtrays, washed up. She moved the chairs in the living room back into their old positions, opened a window and aired the room.

She opened the door to the child's room; the child was just turning over in bed, and one of his toenails, which Bruno had done a poor job of cutting, scratched against the sheet.

Standing at the hall mirror, she brushed her hair. She looked into her eyes and said, 'You haven't given yourself away. And no one will ever humiliate you again.'

She sat in the living room, propping her legs on a

second chair, and looked at the sketch the chauffeur had left. She poured herself a glass of whisky and pushed up the sleeves of her sweater. She smiled to herself and shook the dice cup, leaned back and wiggled her toes. For a long time she sat perfectly still; her pupils pulsated evenly and grew gradually larger. Suddenly she jumped up, took a pencil and a sheet of paper, and began to sketch: first her feet on the chair, then the room behind them, the window, the starry sky, changing as the night wore on – each object in every detail. Her strokes were awkward and uncertain, lacking in vigour, but occasionally she managed to draw a line with a single, almost sweeping movement. Hours passed before she laid the paper down. She looked at it for some time, then went on sketching.

In the daylight she sat in the rocking chair on the terrace. The moving crowns of the pine trees were reflected on the window behind her. She began to rock; she raised her arms. She was lightly dressed, with no blanket on her knees.

Written in Paris during the winter and spring of 1976

And so they all, each in his own way, reflectingly or unreflectingly, go on with their own daily lives; everything seems to take its accustomed course, for indeed, even in desperate situations where everything hangs in the balance, one goes on living as though nothing were wrong.

Goethe, Elective Affinities